The SALMON'S TALE

Poem by Jessie Lendennie

Design by Siobhán Hutson

Published in 2021 by
Salmon Poetry
Cliffs of Moher, County Clare, Ireland
Website: www.salmonpoetry.com
Email: info@salmonpoetry.com

ISBN 978-1-915022-08-0

Cover Design: *Eve Jeanotte & Siobhan Hutson Jeanotte*
Inside design: *Siobhán Hutson Jeanotte*

Salmon logo: *Joe Boske*
The colourized Salmon logo on the front cover was created by Eve Jeanotte

Printed in Ireland by Sprint Print

Salmon Poetry gratefully acknowledges the support of
The Arts Council / An Chomhairle Ealaíon

For all the Salmon Poets of Knowledge

Acknowledgements

The author and publisher of this work wish to acknowledge the support of Ennis Book Club Festival for commissioning this work. They also wish to thank The Arts Council / An Chomhairle Ealaoin for awarding a Commissions Grant to Ennis Book Club Festival, enabling them to commission this work. Our sincere thanks to Dani Gill, Bríd Hayes and everyone at Ennis Book Club Festival. We also wish to thank *The Arts Council / An Chomhairle Ealaíon* for its support over the past four decades and the Salmon Poetry Board of Directors for all of their help and support.

The Salmon

Over a deep pool in the River Boyne hung nine hazel trees which simultaneously produced both flowers and fruit. As the nuts fell into the water they fed the salmon that swam there. For each nut that the fish swallowed a bright spot would appear upon its body. The hazel tree is the tree of wisdom, and the nine trees were the nine Virtues of the Poetic Arts. The hazel nut, being both sweet and compact, is the emblem of wisdom in its most concentrated form. All knowledge of the Arts and Sciences was bound up with eating these nuts, and hence with eating the salmon itself. It was from the accidental tasting of this Salmon of Wisdom that Fionn Mac Cumhaill received his gift of inspiration in the Ossianic legends. There are many other stories which bind the Salmon into the fabric of poetic meaning: it is the King of Fishes; emblem of the element water; it returns mysteriously across thousands of miles of ocean to its spawning ground.

From an early flyer promoting
The Salmon International Literary Journal

The Song of Amergin

I am a stag: of seven tines,
I am a flood: across a plain,
I am a wind: on a deep lake,
I am a tear: the Sun lets fall,
I am a hawk: above the cliff,
I am a thorn: beneath the nail,
I am a wonder: among flowers,
I am a wizard: who but I
Sets the cool head aflame with smoke?

I am a spear: that roars for blood,
I am a salmon: in a pool,
I am a lure: from paradise,
I am a hill: where poets walk,
I am a boar: ruthless and red,
I am a breaker: threatening doom,
I am a tide: that drags to death,
I am an infant: who but I
Peeps from the unhewn dolmen, arch?

I am the womb: of every holt,
I am the blaze: on every hill,
I am the queen: of every hive,
I am the shield: for every head,
I am the tomb: of every hope.

Translated by Robert Graves, *The White Goddess*
(First published by Faber in 1948)

The SALMON'S TALE

I've begun watching clouds.

Ireland's sky is full of them, after all. Visitors say the clouds are lower here, maybe that's why I notice them now, when I never did before. Noticing, too, that I have always lived near water and much of the time under it. Rain is an upside-down sprinkling of sea and shivering of rivers, a mirror of our place, our suspension in time.

Now I have to sit down and talk to you, dear water creature whose name I share. If you have something to share of your world, let me hear it, or would you rather learn what I have done in your name? I would risk a lot in telling you, and you might risk your shimmering movement and fierce eye.

Photo: Jessie Lendennie

"I was summoned,"
said the Salmon.

Oh, I didn't know that you saw it like that, certainly I didn't and how could I? Not my mythology… not my culture, not my burden. I had just left the Thames and everything looked very bright then along the Embankment Walk.

And I've had nothing but the weight
of legend all these long centuries.

Now our history is closely bound, and it is our story – however it may digress and shift and tumble.

In those days, when Galway was sleeping and the Corrib River was a lifelong mission for someone like you, there were empty places on every corner and a rattling of windows at night. Under the Spanish Arch, people gathered to feel the river fly out to the Bay and to die their slow deaths.

From a painting by Madge Hutson

No! It was only the quiet in the deep water that called them, and the waiting for the change to come… The leap, the rebirth, and it did come and maybe you can see it like that.

Well… quietly, and not many people paid attention, but, yes, it was a city slowly drawing its breath and we are still exhaling the consciousness of a time of shattering transition.

And you came, and disturbed my river.

Michael and Tim and I and it was the 1st of August and it was nineteen eighty-one and the hottest summer in years and I thought "huh… it's supposed to be raining." I was thinking of you even then, but didn't know it because I thought that my soul was rooted forever in the arid summer dryness of Arkansas. You weren't there, not even in myth, but you remember it too. The magic, I mean. The Mississippi Delta, and the land that was really sea in the blink of an eye. But here the Corrib became bay, became ocean, and the Silver Salmon was the key that moved the torrent, that touched the storytellers and the poets.

All false human fears that disturb us
and strive to take away our silver souls.

Galway, c1982. The launch of the Rahoon Community Festival. Photos: The Galway Advertiser.
L-R: Michael Reidy, Michael Allen, Fred Johnston,
Helen Lane, Jessie Lendennie, and Monica Ennis

No, we believed in poetry, that's all.

And where did that take you, silly poet?

Only to the next step. The human world, yes, but are we not part of your world, too? Not using you for our own selfish works. Can I just tell you, without your judgement? We have only respect for your spirit and your life.

You barely know me… but tell the story, said the Salmon.

"Michael Allen and Jessie Lendennie, editors of *The Salmon Journal.*"

At *The Galway Advertiser* Offices 1982

Photo: Brenda Fitzsimons

Do you remember when all along the Corrib the streets were empty? When the storms brought the sea inland and no one was there to close the doors. When the Claddagh paths wound around one another and over the bridge into Quay Street and those who were left moved quickly from place to place. You could hear the music, I think. Under the water, about your own business. The music never stopped.

Never stopped, but I didn't listen to that music,
only the rhythm of my own breaths
and my easy flow with the river.

But you were aware of everything on the land, even the poets fishing on the last bridge at midnight.

Ha! I certainly knew those poets. They had more grandiosity than sense, and we would gather under the bridge to laugh at them! But, in truth…

In truth…?

In truth, I could feel their hearts beating for knowledge, and that is the saddest thing. I cannot give my knowledge, no matter how much you poets may want it. I am not you. I am not a "Salmon in a pool"! Poor Amergin, how he tried! So many poets tried to translate his words! As so many have tried to understand me. He was the poet of battle, of strife, of attainment. He was human, or myth, or shapeshifter. He was not Me.

No, no, I understand that. But, you know, with all your years, that the days rush along and the sea ebbs and flows and new poets come and bring their histories forward. New voices, as we say. Did you hear the mermaid poets singing? Have you met a Selkie on the beach?

I have seen Selkies that become land creatures, and I have seen poor poets drowning in Manannán Mac Lir's kingdom. I even heard one reciting "I have heard the mermaids singing, each to each. I do not think that they will sing for me…" Poor fella, indeed. No mermaid songs for him.

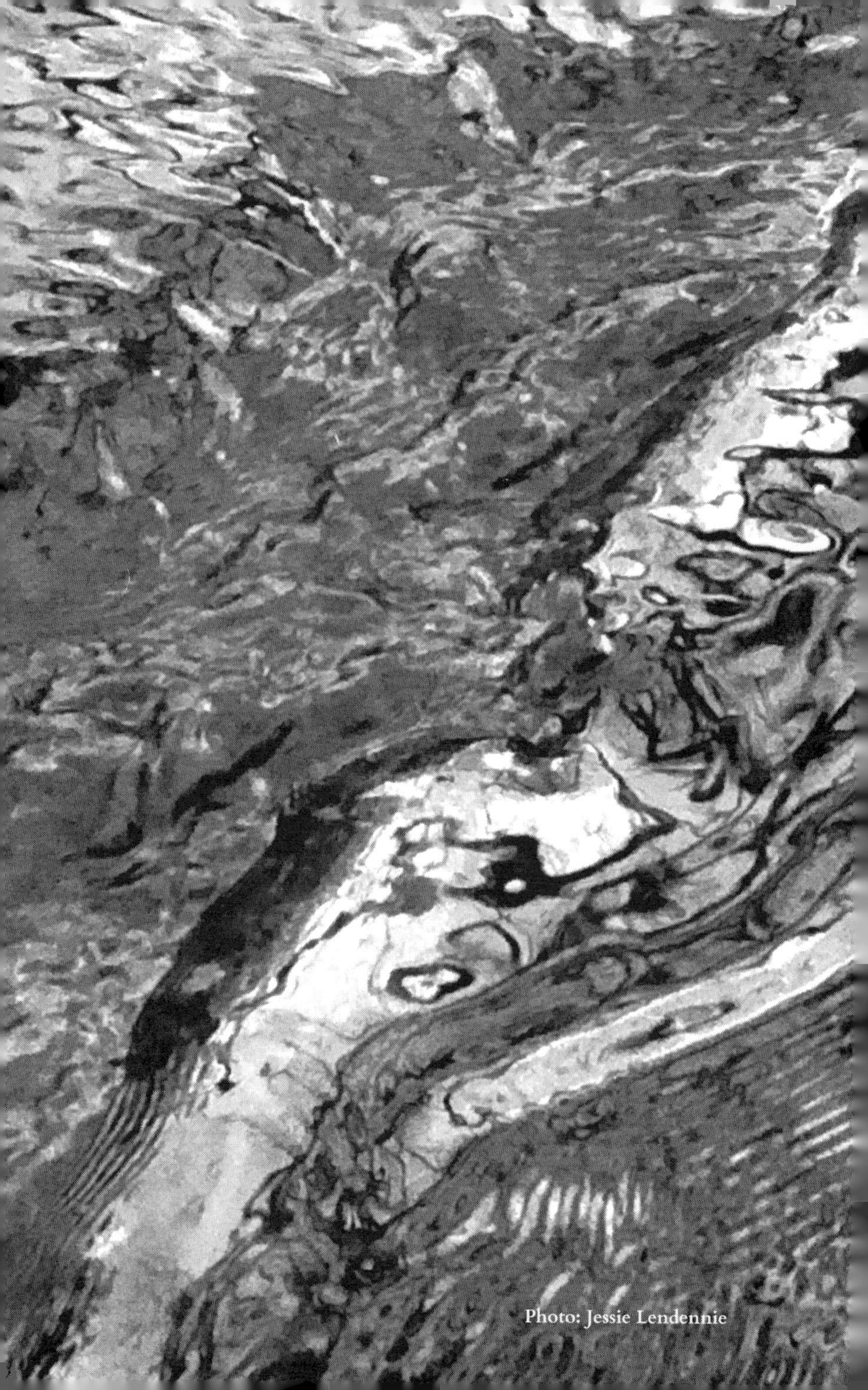

Photo: Jessie Lendennie

That's T.S. Eliot's "The Love Song of J. Alfred Prufrock". How did you hear it?

Poets are always lonely and always talk to the sea, especially the sea within their own souls.

Yes, I think that's true and that's why you are myth and symbol. Sacred to poets.

Oh, no! Never my intention!

Shall I continue with my story, Dear Salmon? I don't mean that Galway was without voice, but it was an understated voice. The voice that builds to the shout of revolution. When Michael and I joined the Galway Writers' Workshop it was just starting, and then the wave came. Do you remember?

What I remember is the sound
of laughter from the river.

One early day, Michael and I walked into the Quay's Pub and I said "Oh, so this is where all the hippies went?" and Michael was embarrassed and there was silence in the pub. Not hippies, I realized, but poets.

Poets disguised as hippies, what an idea!

You're disdainful, but you know that poets keep society, culture, alive. Sometimes you must look carefully for them. They do have disguises at times.

Why look at all? They should
speak from where they are.

Oh, dear Salmon, I know you understand. Shall I continue with my story? There were good writers in the workshop, and it was challenging and exciting. I wondered why more of these writers weren't publishing in journals and making books. It became obvious that there was a split between Dublin and the rest of the country, with Dublin dominating the printed word.

Ah, the Liffey as it flows through Dublin,
too dirty for me. I heard this from some intrepid
fish who had braved the storms of city life.

So, we in the workshop decided to print our own poetry and prose and it was a fine beginning.

Why my name?

After our little poetry chapbook, which we'd called *Poetry Galway*, we knew that we had to take it further and expand into a regular printed journal. And we felt it necessary to have a strong name for an international journal. So, we had a meeting and someone said "how

about *The Copper Salmon*?" and the sound went round the room. What it said was "SALMON SALMON," and I said "Yes, *The Salmon!*" We all said "Yes, *The Salmon*" and we smiled! You must have heard us!

Poetry Galway Issue No. 1, published in 1981, and costing the princely sum of 15p, had cover art created by future Galway Arts Officer James Harrold

From its beginnings, *The Salmon Journal* featured artwork from some of Ireland's most talented artists. This cover image for Issue No.7, entitled "Portrait of J. with Basque beret," is the work of Brian Bourke.

The Salmon is an international literary journal based in the West of Ireland. Since the magazine's first issue in 1981 the editors have worked to establish a reputation for quality of production and content. **The Salmon** includes work from throughout the world but, of course, particularly from Ireland. We publish work in both English and Irish, and also the work of graphic artists and photographers.

The Salmon has published:

the writing of
Ingeborg Bachmann, Eavan Boland, Dermot Bolger, Eoin Bourke, Eva Bourke, Moya Cannon, Michael Coady, Patrick Cotter, Roisin Cowman, Michael Davitt, Gerald Dawe, Louis de Paor, John F. Deane, Patrick Deeley, Eilis Ní Dhuibhne, Michael Egan, Conleth Ellis, Hans Magnus Enzenberger, Gavin Ewart, Gabriel Fitzmaurice, Erich Fried, Paul Ganega, Michael Gorman, Fred Johnston, Michael D. Higgins, Rita Ann Higgins, Ruth Hooley, James Liddy, Thomas McCarthy, Medbh McGuckian, Katherine Machan Aal, Steve McDonagh, Ciaran O'Driscoll, Padraig O'Morain, Gabriel Rosenstock, Anne Roper, Carol Rumens, James Simmons, Knute Skinner, Sydney Bernard Smith, Gerard Smyth, Peter Stinson, Jurgen Theobaldy, and others.

and the graphics of
John Behan, Joachim Boske, Brian Bourke, Christopher Burke, Ann Costello, Eoin Foyle, Anne Kennedy, Jay Murphy, Cormac O'Neill, Mary Redfern, Padraig Reaney, Julian Watson, Carmel Benson, Grainne Dowling and others.

A brochure for *The Salmon International Literary Journal*

I am not angry with you… but you didn't eat the acorns, you didn't taste my flesh, you don't have the knowledge!

I don't aspire to omnipresence, I simply want the path to discovering one's own poetic voice to be easier. Poetry is understanding, not all-knowing. Which is more important? Poetry means to have real knowledge of the world, empathy, beauty, connection, aspiration toward a creative view of the whole. That's what you represent to poets, Fine Salmon.

I did hear you and I came up the Weir and stayed a while to listen for more voices.

Rita Ann Higgins & Jessie Lendennie, The Quays Pub, Galway, 1986

Irish women poets were vastly under-represented in the literary canon and my aim was for women poets to find their voices. Those who were neglected in publishing and, so, neglected by the literary estate. When the books started, the first was Eva Bourke's *Gonella** with lovely illustrations by Jay Murphy.

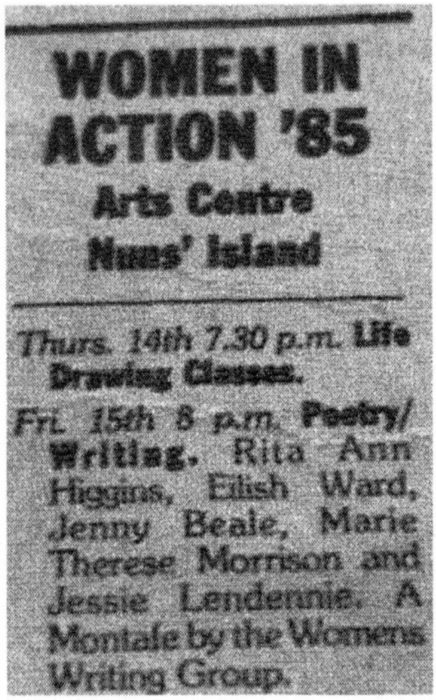
WOMEN IN ACTION '85
Arts Centre Nuns' Island

Thurs. 14th 7.30 p.m. **Life Drawing Classes.**
Fri. 15th 8 p.m. **Poetry/ Writing.** Rita Ann Higgins, Eilish Ward, Jenny Beale, Marie Therese Morrison and Jessie Lendennie. A Montafe by the Womens Writing Group.

Oh, Eva. So beautiful, with her shining hair blowing wild as she walked along the canal. And the artist Jay Murphy with her magic painting. And they made a book and you put my name on the cover.

* *Gonella* by Eva Bourke (1985)

My
old friend Joe Boske
drew an image of me. Joe saw the waves
gathering and it's a good image, but it's not Me. He
told me, one night at the Weir that he didn't want to draw
my essence, so he took an image already known. Remember
Yeats? Did you know him? He chose that image for a coin. New
coins for the new Republic, so I heard. An English artist, so no
chance of capturing my soul. That was good, but I believe Yeats
made a mistake when he called me a "…silver trout" in his
wandering poem. I know he meant Salmon, but he knew
he couldn't catch me, or the rhyme, or the shape-
shifting creature who could never love him.
He was much better with Swans.

Yeats's "The Song of Wandering Aengus". That's a favourite poem for many. It's about beauty, longing, and the unattainable. It does express its purpose.

Poets always chase the unattainable, not the simple appreciation of what is.

To me poetry *is* the appreciation of what is! Please pardon my grammar, this is very emotional for me.

A Silver Salmon
Disrupts the April river
Smiles into the rain

I see, but would you like to be a metaphor?

Not all Salmon are metaphors. Sometimes a Salmon is just a Salmon.

Ha! Ha! Fair point, silly poet!

Well, I'll go on. So much time has passed and so many words. Amazing words, and once they started there was no stopping them. Rita Ann Higgins came along to the Galway Writers' Workshop and everyone knew that she was a unique voice. I knew that she would make a great contribution to Irish literature, and so she has. *Goddess on the Mervue Bus** was groundbreaking and much loved. All the books that have come from her since are welcomed like lifelines.

* *Goddess on the Mervue Bus* by Rita Ann Higgins (1986)

"There are not many books of poems of which I can say that I can remember the day, the month, the year when I read them. Rita Ann Higgins's *Goddess on the Mervue Bus* was such a book. It was a cold dark winter's day when I read it and it lit a fire in my heart. To me Rita Ann Higgins means a unique line in human warmth; and a unique colour of humour and a unique clarity."

Paul Durcan

I heard Rita Ann's voice. I heard her laughing on Long Walk. Dancing with words at the Spanish Arch. I had to stop my music and listen. So much of my dark humour is in her laugh and in her words.

Your music?

Sometimes I say that, among friends. We play and there's always a crowd of sea creatures. Everyone. Even Manannán Mac Lir comes, but he is not musical. We play and sing for our poor sisters and brothers in captivity.

Music is, of course, a form of poetry.

Perhaps the finest poetry and the finest music. So, your story?

After Eva and Rita Ann there were books by Moya Cannon, Mary O'Malley, Joan McBreen, Anne Kennedy.

FROM TOP: Joan McBreen & Jessie Lendennie; Anne Kennedy;
the cover of Moya Cannon's debut collection, *Oar* (Salmon, 1990); and Mary O'Malley

Jessie with Jerah Chadwick, Alaska, 1999, on a promotional tour for Jerah's collection *Story Hunger* and *A Curb in Eden*, a collection by another late Alaskan poet Joseph Enzweiler

And there were some others from across the ocean.
Jerah Chadwick and Patricia Monaghan from the Pacific.
Jerah had stories from Dutch Harbor, Aleutian Islands.
I love those Salmon Tales!

"Illusion Islands, I've heard them called,
As accurate a term as any, remembering
Lava flats from the ferry, black
Expanses above the distant surface.
How as we neared, they flew up,
Not solid ground but seabirds
Thousands skimming and whirling…"

Oh, that's the last stanza from Jerah's "Sudden Landscapes: Unalaska" in his poetry collection *Story Hunger**.

And when he talked about Salmon in his poem, "Returnings", he saw:

"…Salmon rush the stream
into rapids. White wings
of gulls, eagles and ravens
shadow their splashing,
the flash of fins'
riffling circle and streak…"

* *Story Hunger*, Poems by Jerah Chadwick (1999)

That's what we do: Flash our fins and rush the stream to the rapids! These poems make me happy!

I know I shouldn't think that it's amazing that you know these poems, but I do. Jerah would be so moved. When he came to Galway he brought me a native Alaska woodcutting of a Pacific Salmon. He was a poet immersed in land and sea. I miss him*.

I miss him and his kind.

* Jerah Chadwick was the Alaska Poet Laureate from 2004 to 2006. He passed away in 2016.

So many things happened in Galway in my fifteen years there that the memories crowd together. Michael and I separated. Although we'd done a lot together, we'd grown apart. After ten years of publishing *The Salmon International Literary Journal*, I had to let it go to concentrate on publishing books.

In 1991 Siobhán Hutson started working with me at my house on Fairhill in the Claddagh. As Salmon's reputation grew we published more books, several by men, too: Knute Skinner, Fred Johnston, Michael Egan, Ciaran O'Driscoll and Michael D. Higgins.

Photo: Siobhán, Jessie & Zookie, Auburn House, Galway, 1991

Baby Siobhán
and Tim

Gerald Dawe,
Rita Ann Higgins,
Jessie Lendennie,
John Behan

Edna Faye Kiel
& Knute Skinner

Jessie with
Eamonn Wall

The Fisheries Tower, Galway
Photo: Jessie Lendennie

I heard Michael D. at the Fisheries Tower, early one morning, sending a poem for his daughter deep into the heart of the Corrib:

"What value
My distraction
From your task?
Yours was the work of shaping,
Making your own order
In the chaos of others' demands." *

* *The Betrayal* by Michael D. Higgins (1990)

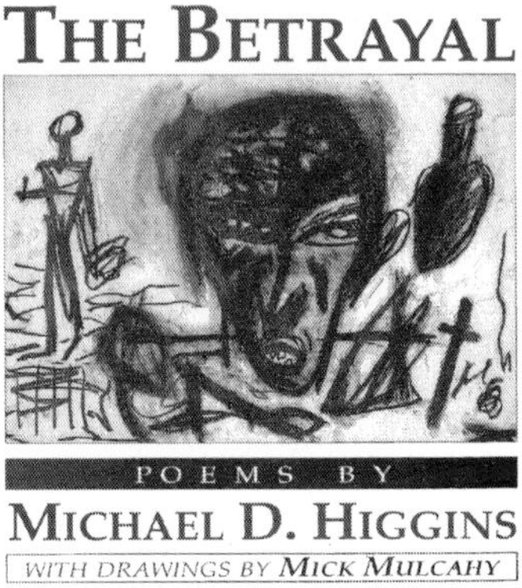

The second stanza from "The Inter" for Alice Mary. Such love in that poem! And his acknowledgement that she must make her own way despite what others may want. When *The Betrayal* was published Siobhán and I had moved the office to a lovely top-floor room in the renovated Bridge Mills. We could see the Corrib flowing under the Wolfe Tone Bridge (I always call it the Claddagh Bridge) and out to the Bay. Salmon Poetry got more and more positive attention and I wanted to do more and more books. I do wish I had your wisdom, but I tried to keep up with expectations and…

The Bridge Mills, Galway

You hit the rapids.

Good way to put it, thank you.

"There are ghosts on Quay Street
Not the Claddagh ghosts
Who looked for company
Late crossings on the bridge
To the old place
But my ghosts
Left behind on Fairhill
Wondering now where I am
Why the light flickered
*Why I can't find my way home."**

You heard me then?

I was there when you said that poem,
in the shimmering light. I know your ghosts
and I knew that you would go on,
even though I could never tell you.

* from *Walking Here*, Poems by Jessie Lendennie (2011)

Illustration by David Hill of Auburn House, The Claddagh, Galway – Salmon's first home

While I may not have your wisdom, I do have your determination, not to mention serendipity and luck. So, leaping over the difficult issues, the story continues. Leaving my Claddagh cottage, I moved to a new place in County Clare in 1995, as you know, near the Cliffs of Moher. How lovely it was to breathe with the wind off the ocean. I used to go across the road to the Cliffs in the morning with my companions, Zookie and Zack. We walked and walked. Did you see us?

I see everything. Those were glorious mornings,
like so many. Did you know that your companions
played with me in the shallows? I am a shapeshifter,
a creature of light. And sometimes I am a sea bird
and sometimes the incoming tide and
sometimes a great black hound.

And so you went to the Cliffs of Moher
and found the path to the sea.

Photo: Brenda Dermody

Yes and Salmon Publishing became Salmon Poetry, so that our message was totally clear. Poets sought us out and we breathed and sailed along! It was well past time for all Irish poets to speak from their own lives, not wait to be plucked up by the hierarchy. Eavan Boland could have rested on her own outstanding reputation, but she focused on encouraging women poets and was an inspiration to dozens of aspiring women writers. She gave Salmon unqualified support.

Oh, my dear Eavan. She was embarrassed for me to call her dear, so it was our secret. I say it to you now because I know you miss her. I hear her voice everywhere.

"This is the hour I love: the in-between,
Neither here-nor-there hour of evening.
The air is tea-coloured in the garden
*The briar rose is spilled crepe-de-chine."**

Oh, that's the first stanza of Eavan's poem "The Women", overflowing with atmosphere and grace. It was published for the first time in *The Salmon* journal in 1986. Her belief in what we were doing was so welcome. In the *Irish Times*, she wrote "The Salmon is beautifully produced and printed… a singularly heartening and attractive little magazine." That at a time when reviewers were still labeling poetry by women as "kitchen sink poetry".

Eavan knew that women are weavers and the keepers of tales. I have known many women who walked in the early morning and recited their lives. These were private lives told only to the wild, to the hedges, to the stone ruins, to the sky, to the concrete, and stars. But they were living poems that needed to be heard by all.

Yes. Yes. Maire Bradshaw was also a trailblazer for Irish women poets. She founded The Cork Women's Poetry Circle and Tígh Filí (Poets' House) and in 1986, with Eavan's encouragement, she published *The Box Under*

* From "The Women" by Eavan Boland, first published in *The Salmon Journal, Issue 16, Winter 1986, 5th Anniversary Issue*

the Bed, an anthology of writing by Cork women writers. Catherine Rose founded Arlen House, a feminist press, in 1975. She published Eavan's groundbreaking collections *In Her Own Image* in 1980 and *Night Feed* in 1982. Glenda Cimino's Beaver Row Press published Paula Meehan's first poetry collection in 1984. Paula is one of the most influential contemporary poets.

With so much strength behind us, we forged ahead in County Clare.

Ennistymon with its history; both turbulent and still. The cascades fierce, exhilarating. Caitlin MacNamara Thomas dancing along the Inagh River, into The Glen and along to Doolin. Always dancing; finding her way. I heard her wandering thoughts. She loved the river's movement and she was happy then.

The Cascades, Ennistymon
Photo: Jessie Lendennie

When I met her son, Colm, he told me that his mother was from Ennistymon. Of course, I knew that her family home was here. She spent much of her youth in Ennistymon, but it's easy to associate her with Wales, and even Italy where she spent her years after her husband Dylan Thomas's death. I was delighted to know that she considered Ennistymon her home. She wrote poetry, but didn't publish. Her youngest son Francesco Fazio wrote "I was well aware that living so close to such an outstanding literary figure as Dylan contributed, consciously or unconsciously to Caitlin's sense of being faulty, defective or not up to standards as a writer or poet."

Caitlin was a special spirit. I see her still.

"Dog Days have begun
They are in full swim.
I have lost count of these long,
Pointless, waiting days
With the regret of the past
Annulling each other
I stand between,
Static, with no volition
To move backwards or forwards.
Never have I been so purposeless,
So without confidence, so without defiance
Or life blood, the urge to do a thing."

She wrote that in 1957, "In Static Danger". It feels despairing, but there's courage, too. She had to have courage to recognize her demons.

But her poetry stayed quiet.

Not forever! Perhaps Ennistymon will hear her again!

Caitlin makes me think of a poet in Sligo. She had a strong, clear voice, and she knew another poet from the Pacific who made waves of words around the world.

Oh! Jean Valentine. Jean introduced me to Adrienne Rich and we did a Salmon book together. That was a great honour. Adrienne was a feminist trailblazer and revolutionary poet.

Adrienne Rich: Selected Poems 1950–1995 (1996)

The Under Voice: Selected Poems of Jean Valentine (1996)

The Salmon Carol Ann Duffy: Poems Selected & New 1985–1999 (2000)

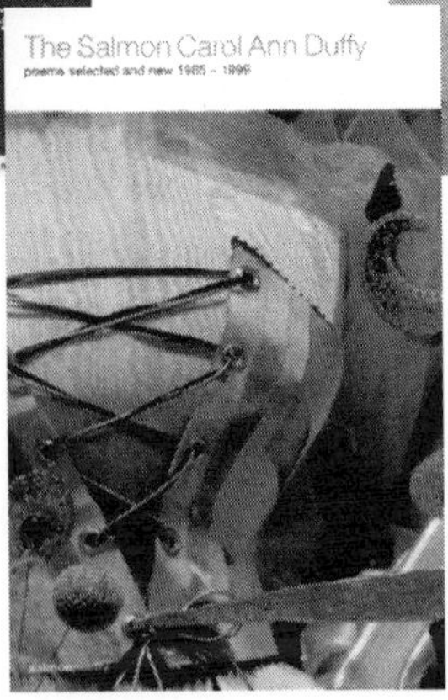

Fierce and wonderful, even for a Pacific creature!

Oh, poetry goes everywhere! It finds its way down crooked roads, into valleys, up mountains, across oceans, and loud highways! It flies into our lives when we least expect it! It called me as a child in Arkansas when I sat in the dirt in front of our house in the cotton fields. "The path is both the horizon and the edge of the sea."

Jessie's parents, Virgil & Willie Mae Lendennie, Blytheville, Arkansas, 1929

I knew you then, even though
all you knew were catfish.
I will have to be on my way soon.
Shall we finish the story?

I understand your time is precious. At the Cliffs of Moher and in Ennistymon, Salmon Poetry grew bigger and bigger. Poets from all the oceans (as you might say) came to us. That's a thrilling thing! And now we have a bookshop in a big house on Parliament Street. The Pacific poet Paulann Petersen reminded me that 'Parliament' comes from 'parler', to speak, thus words, thus the highest form of words, thus poetry! So much serendipity, Dear Salmon.

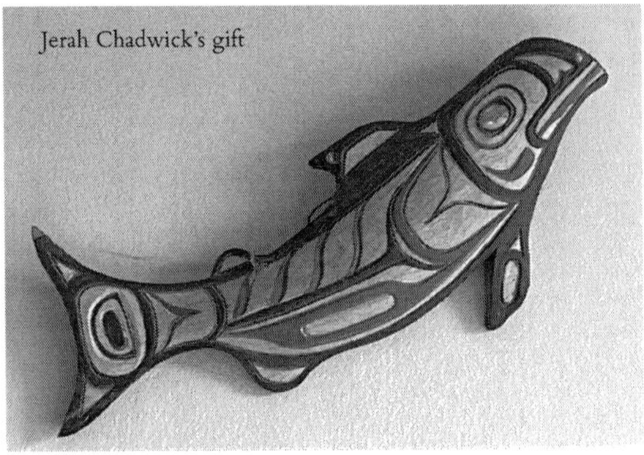
Jerah Chadwick's gift

You seem to have a grá for Pacific poets.

Perhaps. I mention them because they have the feel of Salmon, to complement You.

THE SALMON BOOKSHOP & Literary Centre
The
Salmon Bookshop
& Literary Centre
Parliament Street, Ennistymon, County Clare, Ireland

"Pacific or not, the skies of my heart
are colored by the sea. Color of doves,
they bunch like fleece.
They call to their upper reaches muslin
and linen. They rain. Blackened,
they go, some mornings, all the hues to blue."

Lex Runciman, yes, I can see how you would know him! That's the first stanza of "Pacific or Not", from his Salmon Poetry collection *Salt Moons.*[*]

Lex Runciman
at The Salmon Bookshop
Photo: Jessie Lendennie

[*] from *Salt Moons: Poems 1981-2016* by Lex Runciman (2017)

Did you ever meet another Pacific writer and poet, Ray Bradbury? He wrote many books in his beautiful poetic prose. For some people they were life-changing books. We published his poetry collection *I Live By the Invisible** in 2002. I was introduced to him by a mutual friend, poet Laura Bentley and I found that he had fond memories of when he was in Ireland in the 1950s. Did you ever meet him?

He stayed near the Liffey. I hear him singing
"Swift Hummingbird," although I wasn't there.

The US launch of Ray Bradbury's Salmon collection, *I Live by the Invisible*, Beyond Baroque, Venice, California, 2002

Laura Treacy Bentley
Larry Jaffe
Ray Bradbury
Jessie Lendennie

"You are to me
Calligraphy of God
Whose word
Is symboled on the air for me to read,
The screed and scroll of sky unrolls to see
While everywhere you shape and form the air
Cross section clouds and winds
To circumnavigate my sight,
Only the bumblebee
And dragonfly
Ensnare my eye as you
Do swiftly write invisible words
That that one who
Intuits the heavens, first guesses the blue,
And births the great ox, me
And thistle you.
All joy in a thimble,
I ask for the gist of life,
You paint a symbol,
And leave it to blow on the crystal air,
And go, and lo!
You were never there! *

So many wonderful poets, Dear Salmon. You brought them to us and I will thank you forever!

* from *I Live by the Invisible: New & Selected Poems* by Ray Bradbury (2nd edition, 2008)

Silly poet, gods should never be thanked,
it is in our nature to bestow grace.

Can I send you back to your duties, with an Atlantic poet I believe you love? His words speak to us in the present, but his essence reaches into the unchanging sky.

"It avails not, time nor place—distance avails not,
I am with you, you men and women of a generation, or ever so many generations hence,
Just as you feel when you look on the river and sky, so I felt,
Just as any of you is one of a living crowd, I was one of a crowd,
Just as you are refresh'd by the gladness of the river and the bright flow, I was refresh'd,
Just as you stand and lean on the rail, yet hurry with the swift current, I stood yet was hurried,
Just as you look on the numberless masts of ships and the thick-stemm'd pipes of steamboats, I look'd.
. . .
What is it then between us?
What is the count of the scores or hundreds of years between us?

Walt Whitman, yes!

From "Crossing Brooklyn Ferry", so powerful! I am standing there with him.

I'll leave you to work out your own puzzle, Dear Poet. I heard you in Alaska on Spruce Island and this is the final thing you said in that poem-thought:

Leaving there were Salmon
In a small stream
That rolled down to the beach
Beautiful Salmon
Going home or starting out,
*I had no idea.**

* from *Walking Here*, Poems by Jessie Lendennie (2011)

I may never know.

Sir Silkcoat,
fishing for
Salmon?

Zeke,
Hound of
Salmon

Fionnuala Tuohey,
Jacqui Hersey,
Zeke and Jack
listen to Kevin
Higgins read in
The Salmon
Bookshop Garden

Carolyn Tipton,
Anne Casey,
Sandra Yannone.
AWP Conference
2020

Ray Jeanotte
signing copies of his
book, *The Blues:
A Photographic
Tribute,* at The
Salmon Bookshop
2014

Siobhán & Jessie at
The Salmon
Bookshop &
Literary Centre

River

What keeps the water from being stopped by
the rock? The rock
keeps stepping
over it.

Tess Gallagher

from *Days of Clear Light – A Festschrift in Honour of Jessie Lendennie & in Celebration of Salmon Poetry at 40.*
Edited by Nessa O'Mahony & Alan Hayes (2021)

Salmon Poetry Bibliography 1981-2021

1981-1991	*The Salmon International Literary Journal*	
1986	*We Came Out Again to See the Stars*	Michael Egan
	Goddess on the Mervue Bus	Rita Ann Higgins
	Monkeys in the Superstructure	Peadar O'Donnell
1987	*Gog & Magog*	Ciaran O'Driscoll
1988	*Song at the Edge of the World*	Fred Johnston
	Daughter	Jessie Lendennie
	The Night Parrot	Clarinda Harriss-Lott
	Learning to Spell Zucchini	Knute Skinner
1989	*The Hour of Pan/ama*	Nuala Archer
	Litany of the Pig	Eva Bourke
	The Goose Herd	Roz Cowman
	Striking Water	Paul Genega
	Buck Mountain Poems	Anne Kennedy
	The Salmon Guide to Poetry Publishing in Ireland	Jessie Lendennie
	When You Need Time	Clairr O'Connor
	In Fields I Hear Them Sing	Jo Slade
1990	*Walking the Marches*	Sam Burnside
	Oar	Moya Cannon
	The Ordinary House of Love	Theo Dorgan
	The Betrayal	Michael D. Higgins
	Goddess & Witch	Rita Ann Higgins
	Roman Pines at Berkeley	Hugh O'Donnell
	Reading the Sunflowers in September	Mary O'Donnell
	A Consideration of Silk	Mary O'Malley
	Ireland's Musical Instrument Makers	Joyce Pye
	The Hen Ark	Mark Roper
	Let Live	Eithne Strong
1991	*Strange Bedfellows*	Pat Boran
	Abigail Brown	Heather Brett
	Moving into the Space Cleared by Our Mothers	Mary Dorcey
	Up She Flew	Michael Gorman
	Now is a Moveable Feast	Anne Le Marguand Hartigan
	Face Licker Come Home	Rita Ann Higgins
	Etchings	John Kavanagh
	The Salmon Guide to Creative Writing in Ireland	Jessie Lendennie & Patrick Hickson
	Opposite Walls	Noel Monahan
	In Queen Mary's Gardens	Tom Morgan
	Tipperary	Desmond O'Grady

	The Bears & Other Poems	Knute Skinner
	A Quiet Pint in Kinvara	Richard Tillinghast
1992	*The Hour of Pan/Amá*	Nuala Archer
	Oasis in a Sea of Dust	Vicki Crowley
	Columbus Rides Again	Gerard Donovan
	Philomena's Revenge	Rita Ann Higgins
	Rough Landings	Ted McNulty
	The World Faces Johnny Tripod	John Millett
	The Peacock's Eye	Sheila O'Hagan
	There is Something	Kate Thompson
	Consequences of Slaughtering Butterflies	Olaf Tyaransen
1993	*Silence and the Blue Night*	Angela Greene
	Immortal Sins	Anne Le Marquand Hartigan
	A Smell of Camphor	Breda Sullivan
1994	*Above the Waves Calligraphy*	Patricia Burke Brogan
	Eclipsed	Patricia Burke Brogan
	The Back Road to Arcadia	Michael Heffernan
	This Hour of the Tide	Catherine Phil MacCarthy
	Goldfish in a Baby Bowl	Áine Miller
	Echoes of Memory	John O'Donohue
	What Trudy Knows & Other Poems	Knute Skinner
	Samhain and Other Poems	Robin Skelton
	The Vigilant One	Jo Slade
	Dyckmann--200th Street	Eamonn Wall
1995	*Kings & Bicycles*	Gerard Donovan
	The River that Carries Me	Mary Dorcey
	Rosa Mundi	Theo Dorgan
	A Walled Garden in Moylough	Joan McBreen
	On the Block	Ted McNulty
	Snowfire	Noel Monahan
	The Troubled House	Sheila O'Hagan
	Any Change for the Jugglers	Barbara Parkinson
	The Aphrodite Stone	Janet Shepperson
	Settler	Janice Fitzpatrick Simmons
	Mainstream	James Simmons
	The Under Voice	Jean Valentine
	Tin Drum Country	Sabine Wichert
1996	*The Old in Rapallo*	Rory Brennan
	The New Pornography	Patrick Chapman
	Clearing the Space: A Why of Writing	Anne Le Marquand Hartigan
	Higher Purchase	Rita Ann Higgins
	Selected Poems 1950-1995	Adrienne Rich
	The Cold Irish Earth	Knute Skinner
1997	*Verbum et Verbum*	Mícheál Fanning
	Midcentury	Ben Howard
	Death and the River	Ron Houchin

	True North	Fred Johnston
	The Shadow Keeper	Jean O'Brien
	The Knife in the Wave	Mary O'Malley
	Certain Octobers	Jo Slade
	Today in the Café Trieste	Richard Tillinghast
	Iron Mountain Road	Eamonn Wall
1998	*The White Beach: New & Selected Poems 1960-1998*	Leland Bardwell
	Wednesday: Selected Poems 1966-1997	Marvin Bell
	When It Came Time	Jeri McCormick
	Unlegendary Heroes	Mary O'Donnell
	Journey Backward	Tom O'Malley
	Crossings	Gwyn Parry
	After the Ball	Breda Sullivan
	Weathering	Ann Zell
1999	*The Portable Creative Writing Workshop*	Pat Boran
	The Puzzle-Heart	Louise C. Callaghan
	Story Hunger	Jerah Chadwick
	A Curb in Eden	Joseph Enzweiler
	Kerry On My Mind	Gabriel Fitzmaurice
	The Interior Act	Frank Golden
	Another Part of the Island	Michael Heffernan
	Defining Absence	John Hildebidle
	Falling into Monaghan	Gerard Hull
	Half-Day Warriors	John Kavanagh
	The White Page / An Bhileog Bhán: 20th Century Irish Women Poets	Joan McBreen
	Tenant	Máighréad Medbh
	All the Money in the World	John Menaghan
	Still Listening	Angela Patten
	Starting at Purgatory	Janice Fitzpatrick Simmons
	The Company of Children	James Simmons
	Split the Lark	R.T Smith
	Notes	Peter Van de Kamp
	Terebinthos	Gordon Walmsley
	Sharing Darwin	Sabine Wichert
2000	*The Getting of Vellum*	Catherine Byron
	The Light House	Gerard Donovan
	The Salmon Carol Ann Duffy	Carol Ann Duffy
	The Last Regatta	Maurice Harmon
	Gold Set Dancing	James Liddy
	Little River: New & Selected Poems	Linda McCarriston
	Touchwood	Áine Miller
	Curse of The Birds	Noel Monahan
	Autumn in the Alaska Range	Tom Sexton
	Iced Water	John Unrau
	Sandgames	Michèle Vassal
	The Crosses	Eamonn Wall

2001	*Measures*	Nadya Aisenberg
	Like Joy In Season, Like Sorrow	Mary Dorcey
	The Exile House	Erling Friis-Baastad
	That Fall: New & Selected Poems	Paul Genega
	Airborne	Mark Granier
	Daughter & Other Poems	Jessie Lendennie
	Asylum Road	Mary O'Malley
	A Prayer for Robert Lee	Jude Nutter
	Tulle	Mary O'Donoghue
	Sending Down the Sparrows	Laura Lundgren Smith
2002	*I Live by the Invisible: New & Selected*	Ray Bradbury
	In the Chair: Interviews with Northern Irish Poets	John Brown, editor
	All Things Considered	Mary Coll
	Cape Clear: New & Selected Poems	Theodore Deppe
	The Separation of Grey Clouds	Mícheál Fanning
	Moveable Darkness	Ron Houchin
	Dancing with Chaos	Patricia Monaghan
	The One Who Swears You Can't Start Over	Ethna McKiernan
	Pictures of the Afterlife	Jude Nutter
	Stretches	Knute Skinner
2003	*Stained Glass at Samhain*	Patricia Burke Brogan
	The Middleman	David Cavanagh
	Winter in the Eye: New & Selected Poems	Joan McBreen
	The Drowning of the Saints	Paul Perry
2004	*Libido Café*	Marck L. Beggs
	The Doll with Two Backs & Other Poems	Maurice Harmon
	Dark Pool	Ben Howard
	Taking Time Out	Thomas Krampf
	The Doctor's House: An Autobiography	James Liddy
	The Funeral Game	Noel Monahan
	Black State Cars	Alan Jude Moore
	Sculpture in Black Ice	Breda Sullivan
	Fire & Ice: Nine Poets from Scandinavia and the North	Gordon Walmsley, editor
	Refuge at DeSoto Bend	Eamonn Wall
	The Velocity of Dust	Gary J. Whitehead
2005	*Riverfall*	Simmons B. Buntin
	Remember the Birds	Louise C. Callaghan
	Nourishment	Anne Le Marquand Hartigan
	The Boy with No Face	Kevin Higgins
	City of Bridges	Jo Slade
2006	*Homage*	Mícheál Fanning
	Big Men Speaking to Little Men	Philip Fried
	Selected & New Poems	Robert Greacen
	Cutting My Mother's Hair	Stephanie McKenzie
	She Alone	John Menaghan

2007	*Ancestor Worship*	Michael S. Begnal
	That Morning Will Come: New & Selected	Seamus Cashman
	Breaking Hearts & Traffic Lights	Patrick Chapman
	Twenty-One Sonnets	Gabriel Fitzmaurice
	Anatomy of a Love Affair	Mélanie Francès
	The Sky Road	Mark Granier
	Poems to My Wife and Other Women	Thomas Krampf
	The Boy in the Ring	Dave Lordan
	Digging Up the Boys	Laura Lundgren Smith
	Freshly Rooted	Emily Wall
2008	*Ground Forces*	Paul Allen
	Object Found	Gustáv Báger
	Conflicted Light	J.P. Dancing Bear
	Catastrophic Chords	Marck L. Beggs
	Thornfield: Poems by the Thornfield Poets	Andrew Carpenter, editor
	Catching the Light: Views & Interviews	Gerald Dawe
	Big Pink Umbrella	Susan Millar DuMars
	Tethered to the Earth	Tyler Farrell
	In Daily Accord	Frank Golden
	The Mischievous Boy and other poems	Maurice Harmon
	To Keep the Light Burning	Anne Le Marquand Hartigan
	The Odor of Sanctity	Michael Heffernan
	Finding the Gossamer	Patrick Hicks
	Time Gentlemen, Please	Kevin Higgins
	Signs Translations	John Hildebidle
	Lost in the Gaeltacht	Caroline Lynch
	Polishing the Evidence	Cecilia McGovern
	Lost Republics	Alan Jude Moore
	Green	Patrick Moran
	A Father's Day	Pete Mullineaux
	The Kiss: New & Selected Poems	Ulick O'Connor
	Torching the Brown River	Lorna Shaughnessy
	Seaway: New & Selected Poems	Todd Swift
	In Train	Peter van de Kamp
	A Tour of Your Country	Eamonn Wall
2009	*The Essential Guide to Flight*	Celeste Augé
	Truckers' Moll	Rosemary Canavan
	Falling Body	David Cavanagh
	Long Division	Andrea Cohen
	Are you ready?	John Corless
	Cohort	Philip Fried
	Downstate	David Gardiner
	Standing in the Pizzicato Rain	Georgina Eddison
	At Grattan Road	Gerard Hanberry
	Museum Crows	Ron Houchin
	Leaf, Sunlight, Asphalt	Ben Howard
	Poetry: Reading it, Writing it, Publishing it	Jessie Lendennie
	The Full Shilling	James Liddy

	The Watchful Heart: A New Generation of Irish Poets, Poems and Essays	Joan McBreen
	Heather Island	Joan McBreen
	Grace Must Wander	Stephanie McKenzie
	a compact of words	rob mclennan
	What Vanishes	John Menaghan
	Long-distance Swimmer	Dorothy Molloy
	Lovely Legs	Jean O'Brien
	Along the Liffey: Poems & Short Stories	Sheila O'Hagan
	In Sight of Home	Nessa O'Mahony
	The Follower's Tale	Stephen Roger Powers
	Uttering Her Name	Gabriel Rosenstock
	Starting from Anywhere	Lex Runciman
	St. Michael in Peril of the Sea	Janice Fitzpatrick Simmons
	Human Costume	A.E. Stringer
2010	*Inner City of Gulls*	J.P. Dancing Bear
	Honouring the Word: Poetry and Prose Celebrating Maurice Harmon on his 80th Birthday	Barbara Brown, editor
	Bloom	Simmons B. Buntin
	In the Ninth House	Louise C. Callaghan
	The Darwin Vampires	Patrick Chapman
	To the New World	Valerie Duff
	Where's Katie?	Elaine Feeney
	Free Sex Chocolate	Julian Gough
	Anniversary	Richard W. Halperin
	Blue Abundance	Noel Hanlon
	Beneath a Portrait of a Horse	Cynthia Hardy
	When Love is Not Enough: New & Selected	Maurice Harmon
	Hands Moving at the Speed of Falling Snow	Aideen Henry
	This London	Patrick Hicks
	Frightening New Furniture	Kevin Higgins
	Hurting God: Part Essay, Part Rhyme	Rita Ann Higgins
	One Child Sold: Human Trafficking & Rights	Larry Jaffe
	Prophesying the Past	Noel King
	Dogs Singing: A Tribute Anthology	Jessie Lendennie
	End of American Magic	Christopher Locke
	Invitation to a Sacrifice	Dave Lordan
	In Other Words	Mary Madec
	Dreams for Breakfast	Susan Millar DuMars
	Curve of the Moon	Noel Monahan
	Strasbourg	Alan Jude Moore
	Spear-fishing on the Chatanika	John Morgan
	Zephyr	Mary Mullen
	To The Winds Our Sails: Irish Writers Translate Galician Poetry	Mary O'Donnell & Manuela Palacios, editors
	Heart Turned Back	Bertha Rogers
	The San Simeon Zebras	C.J. Sage
	Find a Place that Could Pass for Home	Glenn Shea
	Help Me to a Getaway: A Memoir	Knute Skinner
	Chopping Wood with T.S. Eliot	John Walsh

2011	*Winter Dogs*	Drew Blanchard
	Kentucky Derby	Andrea Cohen
	Guarding the Flame	Majella Cullinane
	Destiny in My Hands	Primrose Dzenga
	The Mind	John Fitzgerald
	Poems of Faith and Doubt	Gabriel Fitzmaurice
	Early / Late: New & Selected Poems	Philip Fried
	Daytime Astronomy	Paul Grattan
	Unsweet Dreams	Anne Le Marquand Hartigan
	Its Words You Want	Patrick Kehoe
	Kidland and Other Poems	Paul Kingsnorth
	Walking Here	Jessie Lendennie
	Fell Hunger	Joseph Lennon
	Night Walk	John McKeown
	Sky Thick With Fireflies	Ethna McKiernan
	Gods of Babel	Judith Mok
	Session	Pete Mullineaux
	House of Bees	Stephen Murray
	The Juno Charm	Nuala Ní Chonchúir
	The Blue Guitar	Padraig O'Moráin
	As Much As	Allan Peterson
	Stray Birds / Éanlaith Strae	Gabriel Rosenstock
	Witness Trees	Lorna Shaughnessy
	Mad for Meat	Kevin Simmonds
	The Parrots of Villa Gruber Discover Lapis Lazuli	Julian Stannard
	A Taste for Hemlock	Michèle Vassal
	The Geese at the Gates	Drucilla Wall
	Sailing Lake Mareotis	Eamonn Wall
	Ghost Estate	William Wall
	Echoes of a River: Poems of New Orleans and Beyond	Gordon Walmsley
	Silent Music	Adam Wyeth
2012	*Future Blues*	Michael S. Begnal
	home more or less	Paul Casey
	A Promiscuity of Spines: New & Selected	Patrick Chapman
	Thanks for Nothing, Hippies	Sarah Clancy
	Perhaps the Heart is Constant After All	Mary Dorcey
	The Day Judge Spencer Learned the Power of Metaphor	Cynthia Schwartzberg Edlow
	The Land of Give and Take	Tyler Farrell
	Beyond the Sea	Anne Fitzgerald
	Little Murders Everywhere	Rebecca Morgan Frank
	Whatever Sends the Music Into Time New & Selected Poems	Leah Fritz
	Loose Connections	Maurice Harmon
	The Breaking of the Day	Michael Heffernan
	Mentioning the War: Essays & Reviews 1999-2011	Kevin Higgins
	Don't Go There	Colm Keegan
	Selected Poems	Thomas Krampf

	The Sin-Eater: A Breviary	Thomas Lynch
	Where Sadness Begins	John MacKenna
	Jessica Casey & Other Works: Away with Words	Mary Madec, editor
	Marrowbone of Memory	Jeri McCormick
	Empire of Shadows	Hugh McFadden
	The lucky star of hidden things	Afric McGlinchey
	Waiting for Saint Brendan & Other Poems	David McLoghlin
	Forms of Feeling: Poetry in Our Lives. Essays & Interviews	John Morgan
	The Book of Water	John Murphy
	Merman	Jean O'Brien
	Jewel	Peadar O'Donoghue
	We Lit the Lamps Ourselves	Andrea Potos
	Waking Dreams	Donna L. Potts
	The Green-go Turn of Telling	Aimée Sands
	Thousands Flee California Wildflowers	Scot Siegel
	Night Horses	Ilsa Thielan
	Liveaboard	Emily Wall
2013	*Watching My Hands at Work: A Festschrift for Adrian Frazier*	Eva Bourke, Megan Buckley & Louis de Paor
	Circus Europe: Poems and Images — an international collaboration	Machteld Van Buren
	Dangerous to Know	Patricia Brody
	Dreaming My Animal Selves	Hélène Cardona
	Brief Nudity	Larry O. Dean
	The Scale of Things	Edward Denniston
	The Philosopher's Daughter	Lori Desrosiers
	Grass Whistle	Amy Dryansky
	Over the Edge: The First Ten Years	Susan Millar DuMars, ed.
	The Radio was Gospel	Elaine Feeney
	Interrogating Water & Other Poems	Philip Fried
	All I Can Recall	Paul Genega
	Kicking Gravity	Peter Joseph Gloviczki
	Unbelonging	Nicki Griffin
	Shy White Tiger	Richard W. Halperin
	The Quiet Jars: New & Selected Poems	Ron Houchin
	Blue Room	John Kavanagh
	Further Thoughts in a Garden	Rita Kelly
	The Stern Wave	Noel King
	Boogeyman Dawn	Raina J. León
	Saviours in This Little Space for Now Poems for Emily Carr and Vincent van Gogh	Stephanie McKenzie
	Sanctuary	Patricia Monaghan
	Zinger	Alan Jude Moore
	A Shed for Wood	Daniel Thomas Moran
	Night Watchman & Muse	Mark A. Murphy
	On Corkscrew Hill	Stephen Murray
	Any Other Branch	Ivy Page
	The World Shouldering I	James Ragan

	American Dervish	Steven Reese
	The Offspring of the Moon	John W. Sexton
	Concerned Attentions	Knute Skinner
	The Painter's House	Jo Slade
	Late Breaking	A.E. Stringer
	In the Weather of the World	Estha Weiner
	Lit from Below	Terence Winch
	The Hidden World of Poetry	Adam Wyeth
2014	*Skip Diving*	Celeste Augé
	Motherlung	Lisa Marie Brodsky
	The Truth & Other Stories	Sarah Clancy
	Until You Make the Shore	Cameron Conaway
	Favorite Bedtime Stories	John Fitzgerald
	What Our Shoes Say About us	Gerard Hanberry
	Adoptable	Patrick Hicks
	The Ghost in the Lobby	Kevin Higgins
	The Blues: A Photographic Tribute	Ray Jeanotte
	Other Places	Jean Kavanagh
	Memory of Blue	Jacqueline Kolosov
	Lost Tribe of the Wicklow Mountains	Dave Lordan
	Nest	Edward Madden
	Demeter Does Not Remember	Mary Madec
	The World Next to This One	Robert McDowell
	Here and Gone	John Menaghan
	A Thousand Wings	Kelly Moffett
	Where the Wind Sleeps: New & Selected Poems	Noel Monahan
	The Rain on Cruise's Street	Edward O'Dwyer
	Her Father's Daughter	Nessa O'Mahony
	Portal	Mary Pinard
	Commonplace Invasions	Jo Pitkin
	Hello, Stephen	Stephen Roger Powers
	One Hour That Morning & other poems	Lex Runciman
	Bend to It	Kevin Simmonds
	The Shape of the Grave	Laura Lundgren Smith
	Pigment and Fume	Laura-Gray Street
	The Place Where I Left You	Sandra Ann Winters
	Fold of the Map	Joseph P. Woods
2015	*The Conversation*	Judith Barrington
	Blind Verse	Marck L. Beggs
	The Gross & Fine Geography	Stephen Bett
	The Sistine Gaze: I too begin with scaffolding	Seamus Cashman
	Straddle	David Cavanagh
	Evidence of Freewheeling	Trevor Conway
	Papercuts: New & Selected Poems	Bernadette Cremin
	Not Even Laughter	Phillip Crymble
	A Good Enough Love	Owen Gallagher
	The Chivalry of Crime	David Gardiner
	The Night Game	Frank Golden

	Haunt	Mark Granier
	Slow Bruise	Aideen Henry
	Quiet in a Quiet House	Richard W. Halperin
	No Other Gods	Todd Hearon
	Firewood & Ashes: New & Selected Poems	Ben Howard
	Sons	Noel King
	The Rain Barrel	Nicholas McLachlan
	Children's Drawings of the Universe	George Moore
	Bearings	Patrick Moran
	Archives of the Air	John Morgan
	An Unfinished Sufficiency	Ruth O'Callaghan
	An Ink Like Early Twilight	Andrea Potos
	Anchored	Lorna Shaughnessy
	Hominid Up	Neil Shepard
	Junction City: New & Selected Poems	Eamonn Wall
	The Book of Totality	Yun Wang
2016	*Only More So*	Millicent Borges Accardi
	Gynaecologist in the Jacuzzi	Marie Cadden
	Life in Suspension / La Vie Suspendue	Hélène Cardona
	Canal Bank Moon Walk	Alvy Carragher
	Virtual Tides	Paul Casey
	Slow Clocks of Decay	Patrick Chapman
	Sometime I Hear the Clock Speak	Lori Desrosiers
	To Air The Soul, Throw All The Windows Wide	Mary Dorcey
	Bone Fire	Susan Millar DuMars
	American Paprika	Peter Joseph Gloviczki
	Hoops of Holiness	Maurice Harmon
	The Night Watch-man's Daughter	Michael Heffernan
	Little Wanderer	Jennifer Horne
	sombra : (dislocate)	Raina J. León
	Even The Daybreak: 35 Years of Salmon Poetry	Jessie Lendennie, ed.
	Dancing On Top Of A Broomstick	Thomas Lyden
	In A Changing Light	Phil Lynch
	Ghost of the Fisher Cat	Afric McGlinchey
	Driving	Devon McNamara
	How to Bake a Planet	Pete Mullineaux
	The Language Hospital	John Murphy
	Fish on a Bicycle: New & Selected Poems	Jean O'Brien
	Illuminate	Kerrie O' Brien
	Elemental	Ivy Page
	Butterflies of a Bad Summer	Karl Parkinson
	The Pilgrims of Tombelaine	Glenn Shea
	The Constellation of Extinct Stars and other poems	Scot Siegel
	The Fawn Abyss	Adam Tavel
	Granny's Interpreter	Ian Watson
	The Art of Dying	Adam Wyeth

2017	*Lost Addresses*	Diann Blakely
	Activities of Daily Living	Larry O. Dean
	Our Sudden Museum	Robert Fanning
	Squaring the Circle	Philip Fried
	Planet of the Best Love Songs	Ron Houchin
	Allow the Stars to Catch Me When I Rise	Adam Hughes
	Ordinary Gods	Christopher Locke
	The Time of Hunger	Alice Pettway
	Rendering	Jo Pitkin
	Salt Moons: Poems 1981-2016	Lex Runciman
	What the Dust Doesn't Know	Richard Schiffman
	I Offer This Container	Jeffrey Skinner
	Asbestos Brocade	A.E. Stringer
	The Green House	Joyce Sutphen
	The Fawn Abyss	Adam Tavel
	Belfast Notebooks	Jeffrey Thomson
	And There Is Many A Good Thing	Jon Tribble
	Dreampaths of a Runaway	Louise C. Callaghan
	Where the Lost Things Go	Anne Casey
	Prodding the Pelt Cold Weather Anthology	2017
	Rise	Elaine Feeney
	after love	Dani Gill
	gotta get a message to you	Frank Golden
	Ghostlight: New & Selected Poems	Mark Granier
	Trusting Distance	Noël Hanlon
	Flight Paths Over Finglas	Rachael Hegarty
	Song of Songs 2.0: New & Selected Poems	Kevin Higgins
	It's Time	Eamonn Lynskey
	Map & Atlas	Joan McBreen
	Santiago Sketches	David McLoghlin
	Bad News Good News Bad News	Edward O'Dwyer
	Migrant Shores: Irish, Moroccan & Galician Poetry	Manuela Palacios, ed
	Tides Shifting Across My Sitting Room Floor	Anne Tannam
	For Crying Out Loud	Edward Denniston
	Vacant Possession	Anne Fitzgerald
	Will You Be My Friend	Gabriel Fitzmaurice
	Equal Nights	Graham Fulton
	Crossing Places	Nicki Griffin
	After the Fall	Brian Kirk
	Morningrustle	Arno Kramer
	Courting Katie	James O'Sullivan
	Open House	C.J. Sage
	The Yellow House	William Wall

2018	*Birnam Wood / El Bosque de Birnam*	José Manuel Cardona
	To Keep Him Hidden	Ryan Vine
	the gun my sister killed herself with	Daniel Lawless
	The Wounded for the Water	Matt W. Miller
	Stichomythia	Tyler Farrell
	Braille of the Sea	Gordon Walmsley
	The Stone in the Air	Daniel Tobin
	How It Is: Selected Poems	Neil Shepard
	Horn Section All Day Every Day	Cynthia Schwartzberg-Edlow
	Sculling on the Lethe	Paul Genega
	how do i net thee	Shira Dentz
	Whisper of a Crow's Wing	Majella Cullinane
	The Narrow Way of Souls	Eileen Sheehan
	Out of the Ordinary	Moya Roddy
	As Moon and Mother Collide	Mary Melvin-Geoghegan
	Smitten Souls	Gabriel Fitzmaurice
	Catch me While You Have the Light	Richard W. Halperin
	Places to Sleep	Patrick Kehoe
	Wringing Blood: New & Selected Long Poems	Ruth O'Callaghan
	Along the Flaggy Shore	Carlos Reyes
	Songs from the Blue River	Paul Kingsnorth
	Chalk Dust	Noel Monahan
	Afternoon Drinking in the Jolly Butchers	Rachel Coventry
	The Life That I Have	Knute Skinner
	Milking the Sun / Ag Crú na Gréine	Gabriel Fitzmaurice
	The Road, Slowly	Liz Quirke
	Long Love: New & Selected Poems 1985-2017	Judith Barrington
	Randomer	Colm Keegan
	Stopgap Grace	Neil McCarthy
	Ultima Ora	Thomas Kabdebo
	Journey to the Sleeping Whale	Jane Robinson
	Threads	Laurence McKeown
	Our Killer City	Rita Ann Higgins
	Rogue States	Fred Johnston
	Baroque Delights Of Many Layered Petticoats	
	Cold Weather Anthology 2018	
2019	*Fish Singing Foxes*	J.P. Dancing Bear
	Unquiet Remains	Drew Blanchard
	Open Season on the Moon	Patrick Chapman
	Naked: New & Selected Poems	Susan Millar DuMars
	Severance	Robert Fanning
	The Weight of Dandelions	Peter J. Gloviczki
	From the Hotel Vernon	Lea Graham

	Library of the Mind: New & Selected Poems	Patrick Hicks
	How the Weather Was	Jean Kavanagh
	The Fisher Queen: New & Selected Poems	Kathryn Kirkpatrick
	At the Kinnegad Home for the Bewildered	Jeffrey Levine
	Swimming with Shadows	Ethna McKiernan
	The Moving Out: Collected Early Poems	John Morgan
	Guinness on the Quay	Richard Peabody
	One Small Sun	Paulann Petersen
	Moth	Alice Pettway
	All Seats Fifty Cents	Stephen Roger Powers
	Wild Again	Bertha Rogers
	Cycles and Lost Monkeys	Jo Slade
	The Memoir of Mona Lisa and other poems	Su Smallen Love
	The Poet of Poet Laval	Carolyn L. Tipton
	Here Comes the Nightdust	Marc Vincentz
	at the last minute	Estha Weiner
	This is What Happened	Adam Wyeth
	Boats for Women	Sandra Yannone
	out of emptied cups	Anne Casey
	May Day 1974	Rachael Hegarty
	Sex and Death at Merlin Park Hospital	Kevin Higgins
	Zeppelin Vending Machine Manifesto	John Murphy
	The Hollow Woman on the Island	Nessa O'Mahony
	Four Seasons	Paul Balfe
	Notes on a Journey: Cold Weather Anthology 2019	Ruth O'Sullivan, ed.
	Katie: Poems for the Young and Young at Heart	Gabriel Fitzmaurice
	The Egret Lands With News From Other Parts	Mary Madec
	Revenant	Clare McCotter
	Reckonings	Patrick Moran
	deleted	Dairena Ní Chinnéide
	Unportioned: New and Selected Short Poems	Ruth O'Callaghan
	An Upside Down World	Knute Skinner
2020	*The Somnambulist and The Good Life*	David Cavanagh
	The Meeting Place	Dede Cummings
	Keeping Planes in the Air	Lori Desrosiers
	Among the Gliesians	Philip Fried
	Where the Lighthouse Begins	Timothy Houghton
	In the Kingdom of Autumn	Daniel T. Moran
	The Chanter's Reed	James Ragan
	Do Not Touch	Sandra Ann Winters
	Days of Clear Light: A Festschrift in Honour of Jessie Lendennie & in Celebration of Salmon Poetry at 40	Nessa O'Mahony & Alan Hayes, eds.

	A Beautiful Pain	Catherine Barry
	Fox Trousers	Eithne Hand
	Afterwords	Maurice Harmon
	Pathogens Love a Patsy: Pandemic & Other Poems	Rita Ann Higgins
	Silver Spoon	Jessamine O'Connor
	Massacre of the Birds	Mary O'Donnell
2021	*the men I keep under my bed*	Alvy Carragher
	the light we cannot see	Anne Casey
	Light Rolling Slowly Backwards	Ethna McKiernan
	Dead Reckoning	Jude Nutter
	Unsafe	Geraldine O'Kane
	Station Lights	Alice Pettway
	How We Arrive in Winter	Liz Quirke
	Persecution	Sofiul Azam
	Twenty-Six Letters of a New Alphabet	Anne Tannam
	Dancing with Memory	Rachael Hegarty
	Swimming to Albania	Sue Hubbard
	The Salmon's Tale	Jessie Lendennie & Siobhán Hutson
	The Wrong Heroes	Eamon McGuinness
	Ago: Selected Poems	Thomas Dillon Redshaw
	Lark Water	Lorna Shaughnessy
	about:blank	Adam Wyeth
	Moonlight: A Full Moon	Louise C. Callaghan
	Stars Burn Regardless	Jean O'Brien
	The Bird in the Glasshouse	Knute Skinner
	Speech Crush	Sandra McPherson

... to be continued

JESSIE LENDENNIE was born in Blytheville, Arkansas. She is co-founder (1981) and Managing Director of Salmon Poetry, for which she has commissioned and published over 600 volumes of poetry as well as a select list of literary criticism, drama, fiction, memoir and essays. Her own publications include a book-length prose poem *Daughter* (1988), reprinted as *Daughter and Other Poems* in 2001 and a collection of poetry, *Walking Here* (2011). She compiled and edited: *The Salmon Guide to Creative Writing in Ireland* (1990); *Salmon: A Journey in Poetry, 1981-2007* (2007); *Poetry: Reading it, Writing It, Publishing It* (2009); *Dogs Singing: A Tribute Anthology* (2010); and *Even The Daybreak: 35 Years of Salmon Poetry* (2016). Her poetry has also been anthologised in *Irish Poetry Now: Other Voices, Unveiling Treasures, The Attic Guide To The Published Works of Irish Women Literary Writers* and *The White Page/An Bhileog Bhán: Twentieth-Century Irish Women Poets*, among others. Her poems, essays and articles have been widely published and she has given numerous readings, lectures and writing courses in Ireland and abroad, including Yale University; Rutgers University; The Irish Embassy, Washington D.C; The University of Alaska, Fairbanks and Anchorage; MIT, Boston; The Loft, Minneapolis, MN; Café Teatre, Copenhagen, Denmark; the University of Arkansas, Fayetteville; The Irish American Cultural Centre, Chicago and The Bowery Poetry Club, New York City. She regularly attends the AWP Association of Writers and Writing Programs Conference in the US, where Salmon is a prominent presence, having been shortlisted for the Small Press Publisher of the Year AWP in 2015. In 2012, she opened *The Salmon Bookshop & Literary Centre* in Ennistymon, Co. Clare, a vibrant hub for literary events, for writers, readers, students & academics, and the base from which Salmon Poetry runs its publishing operation.

SIOBHÁN HUTSON JEANOTTE was born in London and grew up in Galway. She began working with Salmon Publishing in 1991 and learned about book publishing from the ground up. In 1997, along with her brother Aidan of Solas Web Design, she designed Salmon Poetry's first website – www.salmonpoetry.com – making Salmon only the second book publisher in Ireland to have a website. There are now three websites under the Salmon umbrella: the others are www.salmonpoetry40.com, celebrating Salmon's 40th anniverary, and www.thesalmonbookshop.com which sells a wide range of new & collectable books from the premises of The Salmon Bookshop & Literary Centre in Ennistymon, County Clare. Siobhán is Salmon Poetry's Head of Book Production, Salmon's administrator and is co-director of the company alongside Jessie Lendennie. She designs and typesets the Salmon books and promotional material as well as maintaining the Salmon websites. She began designing the Salmon book covers in 2001 and, to date, has designed 474 covers. She has a First Class Honours Degree in Film, Radio and Television Studies. She lives in Clare with her husband Tim, daughter Eve and their cats. She loves dogs too though.

Inis Mór, August 2021

Knockeven, Cliffs of Moher, County Clare

W. Halperin Gerard Hanberry Manuela Palacios Cynthia Hardy Leah Fritz Andre Potos Donna Potts Scot Siegel Glenn Shea Primrose Dzenga Allan Peterson Drucill Wall John Fitzgerald Joseph Lennon Drew Blanchard Adam Wyeth Paul Kingsnort John McKeown William Wall Stephen Murray Ilsa Thielan Padraig O'Morain Julia Stannard Todd Swift Paul Grattan Nuala Ní Chonchúir Patrick Kehoe Judith Mo Majella Cullinane Kevin Simmonds Rebecca Morgan Frank Elaine Feeney Larry Jaf Noel King Tyler Farrell Sarah Clancy Cynthia Schwartzberg Edlow Peadar O'Donoghu David McLoghlin Colm Keegan Paul Casey John Morgan Thomas Lynch Afr McGlinchey Noël Hanlon John MacKenna Christopher Locke Hugh McFadden Aim Sands Anne Fitzgerald Lori Desrosiers Estha Weiner Patricia Brody Peter J. Glovicz John W. Sexton Hélène Cardona Larry O. Dean Amy Dryansky Ivy Page Jam Ragan Steven Edward Dennist Daniel Thomas Moffett Jo Pitk Joseph P. Wood cqueline Kolos Laura Gray St rt McDowell L Marie Brodsky d Phillip Crymb Ian Watson B McLachlan Ow Gallagher Tre nifer Horne Ada Tavel Marie C homas Lyden Al Pettway Joyce Sutphen Jon Tribble Adam Hughes Jeffrey Skinner Robert Fanni Jeffrey Thomson Richard Schiffman Anne Tannam Dani Gill James O'Sulliv Eamonn Lynskey Graham Fulton Anne Casey Nicki Griffin Brian Kirk Arno Kran John Walsh Thomas Kabdebo Daniel Lawless Daniel Tobin Matthew W. Miller Sh Dentz Ryan Vine Neil McCarthy Moya Roddy Eileen Sheehan José Manuel Cardo Mary Melvin Geoghegan Rachel Coventry Laurence McKeown Michael Hartnett Carlos Rey Alvy Carragher Rachael Hegarty Kerrie O'Brien Liz Quirke Jean O'Brien John Murp Edward O'Dwyer Eileen Sheehan Jane Robinson Jeffrey Levine Richard Peabody L Graham Paulann Peterson Carolyn Tipton Sandra Yannone Marc Vincenz Su Smal Love Clare McCotter Paul Balfe Dairena Ní Chinnéide Timothy Houghton Cather Barry Dede Cummings Geraldine O'Kane Eamon McGuinness Thomas Dillon Redsh

Eva Bourke Michael Egan Rita Ann Higgins Peadar O'Donnell Ciaran O'Driscoll Fred
Johnston Jessie Lendennie Clarinda Harriss-Lott Knute Skinner Nuala Archer Medbh
McGuckian Roz Cowman Paul Genega Kate Thompson Anne Kennedy Clairr O'Connor
Jo Slade Sam Burnside Moya Cannon Theo Dorgan Michael D. Higgins Rita Ann Higgins
Hugh O'Donnell Mary O'Donnell Mary O'Malley Joyce Pye Mark Roper Eithne Strong
Pat Boran Heather Brett Mary Dorcey Michael Gorman Anne Le Marquand Hartigan John
Kavanagh Noel Monahan Tom Morgan Desmond O'Grady Richard Tillinghast Vicki
Crowley Gerard Donovan Ted McNulty John Millett Sheila O'Hagan Olaf Tyaransen
Angela Greene Breda Sullivan Patricia Burke Brogan Michael Heffernan Catherine Phil
MacCarthy Áine Miller John O'Donohue Robin Skelton Eamonn Wall Joan McBreen
erah Chadwick Carol Ann Duffy Adrienne Rich Gabriel RosenstockBarbara Parkinson
anet Shepperson Janice Fitzpatrick Simmons James Simmons Jean Valentine Sabine Wichert
Rory Brennan Patrick Chapman Adrienne Rich Mícheál Fanning Ben Howard Ron
Houchin Jean O'Bri ... ick Tom O'Malley
Gwyn Parry Jessam ... Louise C. Callaghan
Gabriel Fitzmaurice ... avanagh Máighréad

salmonpoetry40

40 Years | 300 Poets | 630 Books

Medbh John Menaghan Angela Patten R.T Smith Peter van de Kamp John Hildebidle
oseph Enzweiler Gordon Walmsley Sabine Wichert John Unrau Tom Sexton Michèle
assal Frank Golden James Liddy Nadya Aisenberg Maurice Harmon Catherine Byron
aura Lundgren Smith Ann Zell Erling Friis-Baastad Mary O'Donoghue Jude Nutter
Mark Granier John Brown Mary Coll Patricia Monaghan Theodore Deppe David
Cavanagh Gerald Hull Paul Perry Thomas Krampf Alan Jude Moore Gary Whitehead
Marck Beggs Seamus Cashman JP Dancing Bear Stephanie McKenzie Robert Greacen
Michael S. Begnal Kevin Higgins Simmons B. Buntin Lorna Shaughnessy Gustav Bager
yler Farrell Philip Fried Emily Wall Dave Lordan Mélanie Francès Nessa O'Mahony
ex Runciman rob mclennan Georgina Eddison John Corless Ron Houchin A.E. Stringer
Gabriel Rosenstock Stephen Roger Powers Dorothy Molloy CJ Sage Bertha Rogers Valerie
Duff Aideen Henry Paul Allen Gerald Dawe Pete Mullineaux Patrick Hicks Caroline
ynch Patrick Moran Ulick O'Connor Cecilia McGovern Andrea Cohen Mary Madec
David Gardiner Celeste Augé Julian Gough Rosemary Canavan Mary Mullen Richard

Eva Bourke Michael Egan Rita Ann Higgins Peadar O'Donnell Ciaran O'Driscoll Fred Johnston Jessie Lendennie Knute Skinner Nuala Archer Louise C. Callaghan Gabriel Fitzmaurice Ethna McKiernan Susan Millar Dumars Medbh McGuckian Roz Cowman Carol Ann Duffy Adrienne Rich Gabriel Rosenstock Kate Thompson Anne Kennedy Clairr O'Connor Jo Slade Sam Burnside Moya Cannon Theo Dorgan Michael D. Higgins Rita Ann Higgins Hugh O'Donnell Mary O'Donnell Mary O'Malley Mark Roper Eithne Strong Pat Boran Heather Brett Mary Dorcey Michael Gorman Anne Le Marquand Hartigan John Kavanagh Noel Monahan Tom Morgan Desmond O'Grady Vicki Crowley Gerard Donovan Ted McNulty John Millett Sheila O'Hagan Olaf Tyaransen Angela Greene Breda Sullivan Patricia Burke Brogan Catherine Phil MacCarthy Áine Miller John O'Donohue Eamonn Wall Joan McBreen Barbara Parkinson Janet Shepperson Janice Fitzpatrick Simmons James Simmons Jean Valentine Sabine Wichert Rory Brennan Patrick Chapman Jean O'Brien John Murphy Edward O'Dwyer Eileen Sheehan Mícheál Fanning Jean O'Brien Leland Bardwell Tom O'Malley Gwyn Parry Jessamine O'Connor Alvy Carragher Rachael Hegarty Kerrie O'Brien Liz Quirke Eithne Hand Ray Bradbury John Kavanagh Máighréad Medbh Peter van de Kamp Sabine Wichert Granier John Brown Mary Coll Michèle Vassal Zell Catherine Ann Byron Mary O'Donoghue Frank Golden Nutter Maurice James Liddy Elaine Feeney Gerald Hull Paul Perry Alan Jude Moore Seamus Cashman Robert Greacen Peadar O'Donoghue Michael S. Begnal Kevin Higgins Lorna Shaughnessy Gustav Bager Dave Lordan Nessa O'Mahony John Corless Dorothy Molloy Aideen Henry Gerald Dawe Pete Mullineaux Caroline Lynch Patrick Moran Ulick O'Connor Cecilia McGovern Mary Madec Celeste Augé Julian Gough Rosemary Canavan Mary Mullen Richard W. Halperin Gerard Hanberry Manuela Palacios Leah Fritz Primrose Dzenga Drucilla Wall Adam Wyeth Paul Kingsnorth John McKeown William Wall Stephen Murray Ilsa Thielan Padraig O'Morain Julian Stannard Paul Grattan Nuala Ní Chonchúir Patrick Kehoe Judith Mok Majella Cullinane Noel King Sarah Clancy David McLoghlin Colm Keegan Paul Casey Thomas Lynch Afric McGlinchey Noël Hanlon John MacKenna Hugh McFadden Anne Fitzgerald John W. Sexton Hélène Cardona Edward Denniston Jean Kavanagh Ruth O'Callaghan Phillip Crymble Ian Watson Bernadette Cremin Nicholas McLachlan Rachel Coventry Laurence McKeown Michael Hartnett Mark Granier Jane Robinson Phil Lynch Jean O'Brien

the arts council an chomhairle ealaíon
funding literature

John Murphy Eileen Sheehan Owen Gallagher Trevor Conway Marie Cadden Karl Parkinson Geoghegan Clare McCotter Paul Balfe Dairena Ní Chinnéide Catherine Barry Geraldine O'Kane Eamon McGuinness Thomas Dillon Redshaw Thomas Lyden Anne Tannam Dani Gill James O'Sullivan Eamonn Lynskey Graham Fulton Anne Casey Nicki Griffin Brian Kirk Georgina Eddison Arno Kramer John Walsh Thomas Kabdebo Neil McCarthy Moya Roddy Eileen Sheehan José Manuel Cardona Mary Melvin Geoghegan Clarinda Harriss-Lott Jerah Chadwick Joyce Pye Richard Tillinghast Michael Heffernan Robin Skelton Ben Howard Ron Houchin Marvin Bell Jeri McCormick John Menaghan Angela Patten R.T Smith John Hildebidle Joseph Enzweiler Gordon Walmsley John Unrau Tom Sexton Nadya Aisenberg Laura Lundgren Smith Erling Friis-Baastad Patricia Monaghan Theodore Deppe David Cavanagh Thomas Krampf Gary Whitehead Marck Beggs JP Dancing Bear Stephanie McKenzie Simmons B. Buntin Tyler Farrell Philip Fried Emily Wall Mélanie Francès Lex Runciman rob mclennan A.E. Stringer Stephen Roger Powers CJ Sage Bertha Rogers Tyler Farrell Valerie Duff Paul Hicks Andrea Gardiner Donna Peterson Kevin

salmonpoetry40

40 Years | 300 Poets | 630 Books

Allen Patrick Cohen David Potts Allan Simmonds Scot Siegel Glenn Shea John Fitzgerald Joseph Lennon Drew Blanchard Todd Cynthia Hardy Andrea Potos Todd Swift Rebecca Morgan Frank Larry Jaffe Cynthia Schwartzberg Edlow John Morgan Christopher Locke Aimée Sands Lori Desrosiers Estha Weiner Patricia Brody Peter J. Gloviczki Larry O. Dean Amy Dryansky Ivy Page James Ragan Steven Reese Terence Winch Mark Murphy Raina J. León Daniel Thomas Moran Edward Madden Cameron Conaway Kelly Moffett Jo Pitkin Joseph P. Wood Mary Pinard Ray Jeanotte Jacqueline Kolosov Laura Gray Streete Kathryn Kirkpatrick Robert McDowell Lisa Marie Brodsky Sandra Ann Winters Judith Barrington Neil Shepard Yun Wang Todd Hearon Stephen Bett Millicent Borges Accardi Jennifer Horne Adam Tavel Diann Blakely Alice Pettway Joyce Sutphen Jon Tribble Adam Hughes Jeffrey Skinner Robert Fanning Jeffrey Thomson Richard Schiffman Daniel Lawless Daniel Tobin Matthew W. Miller Shira Dentz Ryan Vine Carlos Reyes Jeffrey Levine Richard Peabody Lea Graham Paulann Peterson Carolyn Tipton Sandra Yannone Marc Vincenz Su Smallen Love Timothy Houghton Dede Cummings